LAST
DAYS
HERE

ERIC CHOCK

Bamboo Ridge Press
1990

This is a special double issue of *Bamboo Ridge, The Hawaii Writers' Quarterly*, No. 45 and 46, Winter and Spring 1989-1990, ISSN 0733-0308.

ISBN 0-910043-18-3
Copyright 1989 Bamboo Ridge Press
Indexed in the American Humanities Index
Indexed in the American Index of Periodical Verse
Copyright 1989 Eric Edward Chock

Published by Bamboo Ridge Press
Special Consulting Editor: Stephen H. Sumida
Managing Editors: Mavis Hara and Kelly Okada
Cover and Book Design: Gary N. Nomura
Cover Art: Doug Young
Typesetting: Gail N. Harada

Some of the work in this issue has been previously published in *Bamboo Ridge, Chaminade Literary Review, Hawaii Review, Talk Story, Seattle Review, The Paper, The Journal of Ethnic Studies,* and *ZYZZYVA*.

———

Bamboo Ridge Press is a non-profit, tax exempt organization formed to foster the appreciation, understanding, and creation of literary, visual, audio-visual and performing arts by and about Hawaii's people. Tax-deductible contributions are welcomed.

Bamboo Ridge, The Hawaii Writers' Quarterly is supported in part by grants from the State Foundation on Culture and the Arts (SFCA). The SFCA is funded by appropriations from the Hawaii State Legislature and by grants from the National Endowment for the Arts. This issue is also supported in part by a grant from the National Endowment for the Arts (NEA), a federal agency.

Bamboo Ridge Press is a member of the Coordinating Council of Literary Magazines.

Subscriptions to *Bamboo Ridge, The Hawaii Writers' Quarterly* are available for $12 a year for individuals, $16 a year for institutions.

Bamboo Ridge Press
P.O. Box 61781
Honolulu, Hawaii 96839-1781

10 9 8 7 6 5 4 3

Thanks to all those who have influenced my writing over the years, especially to the ongoing support of Study Group, to all my family, and to Ghislaine.

CONTENTS

IN A
LULLABY

IN A LULLABY

The burn of sunset
filters through the leaves
of the dragon eye tree
and flashes in her hair
as she weeds the needles
of the Japanese grass
she grows like a futon for me
to stretch my body across
when the sky turns light purple,
or maybe she calls it
some fancy name
like magenta, or violet,
before the first stars
blink for us
through their veil of sky.
I roll over and watch her
purple and orange epidendrums
as she waters their faces,
and we learn to follow hers
as she turns and hums
some old-time melody
her voice fluttering up and down
the notes and through the house
so I can hear it
even if I've gone inside
to set the forks and plates
and cups on the table.
She comes and stands next to me
at the kitchen window,
and in that moment I learn to see
the glitter in the harbor
by looking past the curls
of her hair,
by looking past
her dark brown eyes
that catch the last daylight

before she turns around
to serve dinner.

CONFESSION

I thought we were poor, our family.
There were so many things I couldn't have,
like the lacquered bamboo fishing pole twelve feet long
that could hold the bait out far enough
to where the big ones lived,
deeper than I could see;
or the bicycle I rode down the hill
in my dreams, before I ever knew how;
or the pure white racing pigeon
who almost flew away, but who stayed
and hatched me half a flock
that we could carry by car
to the other side of the island,
and still they'd beat us home.

All these things somehow gave me courage
to sit on the edge of my mother's bed
and calmly tell her why we didn't need
any more babies in our family.
I was sincere. Almost pleading.
But she just acted like she had been waiting
all her life to answer me.
She just looked at me, almost sadly,
and said that when people have babies
it just shows how much they love each other.

I wanted to die.
How could I have known that, in time,
all those things I wanted would come to me?
At that age, how could I know the meaning of babies?
All it made me realize was the meaning
of her breasts when, accidentally
I saw her that time,
silhouetted against the afternoon light
that glowed in the Venetian blinds
and into my eyes, her hair falling

across her bare shoulders
as she toweled it dry before
my father came home.

DANNY BOY

To me it was a Hawaiian song,
as every night your Chinese tenor rose
and filled my two sisters and me
with summer in the meadow;
and with valleys hushed and white with snow
you tucked the three of us in,
your silhouette framed in the doorway briefly
before you finished the song down the hall
only four or five daddy long legs steps away.
Danny was your friend,
and I never knew where he went
or why he left such a sadness
in your voice.
But listening to your big feet
making the hallway creak the short distance
to where mommy waited,
putting her hair in curlers,
newspapers blanketing the foot of the bed,
I felt that even a small good-by
was like a dark bedroom, waiting
for the morning to bring the singer
back to the love of his song.
Outside, a cricket vibrated
through the mock orange hedge,
and after a long trill,
listened—
and started calling again
into the silence.
On the other side of the house
under the banyan tree,
a bullfrog clucked one breath so long
it circled the pond, the house,
and the monkey pod trees, before
he let it fall across the water.
And then we all listened.
Down the hall, the door closed,

the lights went out,
and I fell asleep like the lone singer,
knowing my dreams would always end
I love you so.

THE MANGO TREE

"One old Chinese man told me," he said, *"that he like to trim his tree so da thing is hollow like one umbrella, and da mangoes all stay hanging underneath. Then you can see where all da mangoes stay, and you know if ripe. If da branches stay growing all over da place, then no can see da mango, and da thing get ripe, and fall on da ground."*

And us guys, we no eat mango that fall down. Going get soft spots. And always get plenty, so can be choosy. But sometimes, by the end of mango season when hardly get already, and sometimes the wind blow 'em down, my mother, sometimes she put the fall down kind in the house with the others.

I was thinking about that as I was climbing up the tree. The wind was coming down from the pali, and I gotta lean into the wind every time she blow hard. My feet get the tingles cause sometimes the thing slip when I try for grip the bark with my toes. How long I never go up the tree! I stay scared the branch going broke cause too small for hold me, and when the wind blow, just like being on one see-saw. And when I start sawing that branch he told me for cut, the thing start for jerk, and hard for hold on with my feet. Plus I holding on to one branch over my head with one hand, and the fingers getting all cramp. My legs getting stiff and every few strokes my sawing arm all tired already, so when the wind blow strong again, I rest. I ride the branch just like one wave. One time when I wen' look down I saw him with one big smile on his face. Can tell he trying hard not for laugh.

He getting old but he spend plenty time in that tree. Sometimes he climb up for cut one branch and he stay up for one hour, just looking around, figuring out the shape of the tree, what branches for cut and what not for cut. And from up there can see the whole valley. Can see the trees and the blue mountains. I used to have nightmares that the thing was going erupt and flood us out with lava, and I used to run around looking for my girlfriend so she could go with us in our '50 Dodge when we run away to the ocean. But I never did find her and I got lost. Only could see smoke, and people screaming, and the lava coming down.

The nightmare every time end the same. I stay trapped on one trail in the mountains, right on one cliff. Me and some guys. The trail was narrow so we walking single file. Some people carrying stuff, and my mother in front of me, she carrying some things wrapped in one cloth. One time she slip, and I grab for her, and she starting to fall and I scream "Oh no!" and then I wake up. And I look out my window at the mango tree and the blue mountains up the valley. The first time I wen' dream this dream I was nine.

Since that time I wen' dream plenty guys falling off the trail. And plenty times I wen' grab for my mother's hand when she start for fall. But I never fall. I still stay lost on the cliff with the other guys. I still alive.

And my father still sitting in the mango tree just like one lookout, watching for me and my mother to come walking out of the mountains. Or maybe he stay listening to the pali wind for the sound one lady make if she fall. Or maybe he just sitting in his mango tree umbrella, rocking like one baby in the breeze, getting ripe where we can see him. And he making sure no more extra branches getting in his way.

THE TUNNEL

The concrete pipe in the stonewall gave birth to the stream
as mysteriously as mothers to babies.
By the time we were four it was a great place to hide.
To do dirty things in the dark.
We got in and crawled through spiderwebs,
skinny feet and arms like frog legs
pushing sideways against the curved walls,
above the tubular streambed.
But the big kids came looking and we were trapped.
We knew the pipe started somewhere else
but a hundred yards is a long way in a tunnel with no light.
And they could wait us out near the opening
while we worried about centipedes and scorpions further in
who had ways to find us without eyes.
We wished that we had no eyes either,
that our bodies would grow feelers sensitive enough
to shape the darkness of that disappearing tunnel.
We went all the way into the pipe.
When we were four we found the other end,
a tongue of sun pushing the water beneath us,
forcing light into our eyes.

ALLOWANCE

It wasn't the amount, Daddy.
Five cents a week could've been enough
if I wanted to stretch the pennies
in your dresser ashtray back then,
when even lunch money was hard to find
if you were trying to buy a house
and raise a local family in Hawaii
after the Big War.
But still I wanted more,
a little boy just barely tall enough
to tip toe my eyes
to the level of the dresser top
and curl my skinny arm over the edge
to pluck a silver dime
I hoped hadn't been noticed
among the brown pennies
filling the dish
like so many old monkey pod leaves
waiting to be burned.
More carefully than any game of fiddlesticks
I moved nothing from its place,
the quiet scrape of coins
grating in my heart,
the ashtray unmoved from its station
near the stack of unpaid bills,
your roll-up metal measuring tape,
the Elgin watch you hardly used,
and sometimes during a peaceful late afternoon
you'd lie on the bed
in the darkened room after work,
thin lines of sunlight glowing
on the Venetian blinds,
and I would pretend you didn't hear me
coming and going from your rest,
as you would pretend too.

THE BELT

As I dressed for dinner tonight
I realized I was putting Daddy's
genuine snakeskin belt around my waist,
the one he used to feel was light enough
to wrap once around his fist
and with the free end hanging
whip my small child's body
around my bare legs
as I would run past him after sundown
late from finishing a football game
or wandering too long down an unexplored
tributary in the stream,
not even caring whether I missed dinner
which was nothing
on his plantation worker's salary.
I wonder if he felt
like the man on the horse then,
or if it even entered his mind
what he was passing on to me.

PULLING WEEDS

Dirt sticks under fingernails
harder than penny-a-weed,
and my young knuckles ached
pulling against those roots.
I worked hard as you did
(though you earned twice as much),
but so much crabgrass and nutgrass
littered our dream of lawn;
or was that some lesson in survival
through hard work in plantation fields
which you were passing on to me?
No television, no ice cream,
no nickel for candy that rots
teeth quicker than chewing
sugarcane or mangoes.
This is my heritage,
dirt in my nails,
a natural taste in my mouth,
and you stood over me
like the white man you hate
in your dreams.

CANDY FOR COCO

Every kid
deserves a piece of candy.
So after school,
the ones who could
stopped at the store
and pored over the variety
of sweets, giving back
the nickels and dimes
our fathers had been traded.
Sometimes, if I were lucky
I'd go in.
I remember once,
outside, someone put a
pocket knife point
gently into my back
for a piece
of what I'd bought.
After I gave him some
he became my friend,
even when I had
nothing to share.

Every kid
knows how to share
nothing.
You just walk
with your friends
into the store
and someone asks the owner
about the prices he wants
you to share with him,
as if you were all
born equal.
By the time
the ring of metal
drawers and bells

on the register
full of loose change
stops rattling his skull,
someone else is outside
with your share.

We knew something
was not quite right,
but the sweet taste
in our young mouths
was the American way of life.

OFFERTORY

When you were eleven
and poor,
the green corner
of a one dollar bill
sprouting from the slot
of the offertory box
in the Soto Mission
was temptation enough
for you to take, right
from under the nose
of the compassionate Buddha.
Because you didn't believe in him
you calmly walked out
and spent that bill
at the candy store,
licking ice cream while
down the block he sat,
gold-faced, serene,
content that the brief
Sunday visit you paid him
fulfilled your needs.
But your brother believed
and told your mother,
and you cried when you had to repay
your small boy's good fortune,
your childhood dream
of the sweet life
hardening in your heart
like a stone outweighing the honor
of a whole tradition.

LOOKING BACK FROM A SMALL HILL
TO DOWNTOWN HONOLULU

An old dirt road connected our homes
with a medial strip of blackened weeds
that each of our families greased in common
tickling the underbellies of our primitive machines.
Daddy drove our jalopy jeep slow
to savor each bump, making me
rise, for an instant, tall enough
to see ahead through the windshield
to where weeds ended in a road paved
with oil, greased so smooth
I could see how easy it would be for us
to get to that ocean that, from here,
seemed ready to spill
into downtown Honolulu.

But he always knew better. That water
sparkled with circular rainbows that leaked
from ships, through the harbor.
So he turned our backs on the town
and drove us across the snake that wriggles
over the Pali. The road must have lived then,
its dotted white backbone almost hidden
by giant hanging philodendron vines,
elephant ears in the trees,
and at the meanest turns the wiggly arrow
"snake signs" he told us they were.
They say there were no snakes in Hawaii then.
Not even in the zoo in Waikiki.
But knowing they existed elsewhere
in the world, we headed for the country,
found dirt roads to beaches of the windward side,
and waited for someone to hook by mistake
a pale blue-skinned "white eel"
which swallows the baited hook whole
and ties its body in knots of panic
tangling the lines. Pretending snake,

we'd tease and torture the eel
with knives and spears when it landed.
All dead eels stink. White eels at least
you can give to the old Japanese men to eat.
But if none of the few who knew how
wanted to trouble themselves with all the
skinning, cleaning, the preparation to make it
into a suitable meal, we'd kill it
there in the sand, and leave it for
the crabs, and waves, or maybe for
some fisherman to strip into bait.

Riding back at the widening end of one of those days,
the jeep grinding through the sand and tall weeds
bouncing me and the fishing gear to my last
backward glimpse of the open sea,
the long bamboo poles strapped but jiggling
alongside the jalopy, sometimes I'd pretend
I was a foot soldier in World War II
claiming the beach, for our side, for Hawaii.
We hadn't lost it then,
and could drive the black snake home,
up the dirt weed road, to the homestead.
Above the harbor full of ships
I'd wash off the knives and spears and poles
with fresh water.

TERMITES

They swarm on summer nights.
They seem to come out of the ground,
out of trees, they fill the air.
They've kept their wings
all their lives
folded on their backs,
but in these insect starbursts
they fly toward whatever shines
in street lights, headlights,
reflections in windows, or eyes.

We turn off the lights inside.
We watch as toads
gather at the porch light
and lick themselves silly.
Lizards haunt the windows,
stalking the winged or wingless bodies.
If the creatures get in
we have candles flaming,
or white bowls of hot water
grandma leaves under a lamp
in a darkened room.
Looking out from the window,
it seems as though they're all bent
on living in our home.

On summer nights, thousands of wings
form feathery wreaths
around each house.
Some of these have made it.
But out in front
under the street light
mother shoots water like a gunner,
picking off stragglers
with the garden hose.

LILY POND

He crawled in the river grass
stalking the fish
he believed couldn't see him
through that invisible skin
they lived beneath.
But blurred as their vision would be,
they must have seen his brown face,
sunburned hair gleaming
above cheeks and eyes
that spent hours studying
the way water wrinkled
and cleared
on its steady downstream path
to the sea.
As he crouched among
the fuzzy, knife-edged leaves
he observed their habits,
the way they would drift
in two's or three's,
the way they would nibble
what came within their reach,
unless it made too loud a splash
sending them into the deep,
where they could gather strength
from the dark soft
belly of the stream.

Then it was like they were praying.
Like when there is nothing else
but the anxious feelings
that come from somewhere inside,
and all you can do
is go to that place
where you're alone
with the depth of the water
and the dark shapes

that eventually rise
to the blurred vision
of the one who waits.

When they come face to face
the tension on the water
will wrinkle and clear
till there is nothing between them,
nothing that can break
between the eyes of fish
and the eyes of a boy
who one afternoon
have come together
and prayed.

THE
MEANING
OF
FISHING

II

THE MEANING OF FISHING

You know when you go fishing and you whitewash,
nothing,
you know da feeling, right?
You no can even say was too small
and you threw em back.
At least if you wen hook em,
if you wen feel da muscles of something big
pulling your line out to the ocean,
den you would feel good!
But even den,
if you never land em, no count eh?
No matter how close you brought em in,
even if you saw da blue scales
shining in da shorebreak,
even if you wen drag em up on da sand,
still yet—if got away
you whitewash.
Even if you woulda let em go anyway
after you caught em,
if you never catch em
and hold em in your hands,
you think you know da meaning of fishing?

MAKING DA SCENE

In '66, our hair
was hitting da tops of our collars
and doing da surfa flip,
we neva tuck in da tails
of our button-down paisley shirts,
and you could still wear Beatle boots
and make da scene.
All summer we cruised Ala Moana,
Conrad and me, new wrap-around
sunglasses making everything green,
rolling along with da Stones and
getting no satisfaction
in his brother Earl's '63 Dodge Dart,
lifted, quad carburetor, could do 90
on da new H-1 Freeway, but
we neva even think we was mean.
Everytime around,
we just leaned down in his
blue vinyl seats, hoping
somebody would notice us
as we rumbled through da park,
those wrap-arounds like protection
and a tease
for those cute chicks
who was out there every day,
doing da same thing.

SUCH WINGS

When you touch me
the smoke of dreams
burns through your fingers
and like a cocoon unravelling
the vain center trembles
knowing you love to unwrap
such wings as these thin bones
are growing.

WE KNEW

When I was in kindergarten
it happened.
From beneath the flutter
of straight black hair
a face shined inside mine.
And I felt mine
shine inside hers
as we giggled in recognition.
Even then we knew.
We looked as long as we could,
then continued on our ways.
Later, during recess
under the monkey pod tree
we memorized each other's names
in the soft child's lips
that kissed the other's cheek.
We loved the sweaty heat
that stayed in our hands
after the bell had rung.
It was all we had to do.
As close as two could come.

I just wanted to hang around
and feel good.
I wanted to savor
what little I knew.
It was a kind of mood.
The kind that makes me
sit here tonight
and smile at my salmon steak,
watching the flesh
break apart on my plate.
No one needs to know
the look I saw in you,
the knowing smile
of the child now grown

telling me what I had known
all along is true.

TEA AFTER FISH

When I pour tea, steam rises
like clouds from a hot waterfall,
rises in coils
swirling out of the cup.
The fingers that spun this cup
knew these circles of tea
would fill it,
knew these patterns of steam
would rise into my hair
as I lean over, blowing
into the hollow
between my thumb and forefinger.
As I drink the tea
the fish taste washes into my belly,
and my mouth is fresh
as the green leaves
soaking at the bottom.
The fingers that picked the tea
knew I would smile confidently
near the face of my lover, thinking
of the fish in her stomach,
and the clean taste of tea
on her lips.

THE DOVES

The doves are cooing again outside the window.
He announcing he loves her more than
the brown dry stalk he brings her,
she murmuring yes yes as she tucks
their dream of nest beneath her
dove-soft belly down, sitting just so
the curved stem will stay snug,
but it won't yet, the ledge under this eave
is too narrow to hold them both,
so he sits on her folded wing tips
above her tail, as they watch the nest
slipping away this gentle morning.
In a while he'll notice the mess,
or maybe it's she who nudges him above her,
and he'll fly across the street
for more material, a fresher piece,
anything to make her think
they have a chance in this eave
outside this window where they've watched us
after the same dreams.

3 A.M. WAIKIKI

Coming over the curve of East Oahu
I see your lights red in the clouds
long before the skyline of concrete Christmas trees
appears like the tv backdrop to Dragnet.
Where are you all coming from anyway?

I mean,
I can understand a flock of blind moths
or swarms of lost termites
chasing after the fire.
I've seen cats howl out their territory
or eels cruising between reefs
hoping for a stray meal
or another eel to tangle with.
I know animals move with the moon.

But how do you explain the electric jungle,
the worship of an artificial life
that asks for the recognition of no time,
no natural meaning of the dawn,
no desire for a spontaneous
coming of light?

At 3 a.m. you squeeze the grease
from a billion pre-historic bodies
to light your own; but every night
you squeeze a little closer
to yourself, your time, and when it
comes your turn to be somebody's light,
do you want to be a radiation
into the night waters for chasing eels,
every night, chasing eels?

STILL FISHING

The last time I even tried
to catch anything
that would give itself
up for me
was so long ago
I can't remember.
But what I remember
is enough for me
to believe
I'm still a fisherman.
Most of all
it's the habits
I memorized: patterning
my sleep after them;
learning to catch
and eat
what a bottomfeeder
would muzzle out
with its tough lips
in the sand;
quickly picking off
whatever silver flashes
nearby.
I even had the indecency
to lay in wait
during mating seasons,
taking advantage
of the kind of frenzy
that leaves so many
easy prey.

Maybe it's all these habits
that have made me
keep to myself lately.
But I can hardly go a night
without the smell of the sea

suddenly appearing
in my nostrils;
the tides and moon
move my moods;
and every night
I hold the hook
firmly in my hand,
the surprised body
frantic with a power
I learned with each cast
more and more
to feel.

THE BAIT

Saturday mornings, before
my weekly chores,
I used to sneak out of the house
and across the street,
grabbing the first grasshopper
waking in the damp California grass
along the stream.
Carefully hiding a silver hook
beneath its green wings,
I'd float it out
across the gentle ripples
towards the end of its life.
Just like that.
I'd give it the hook
and let it ride.
All I ever expected for it
was that big-mouth bass
awaiting its arrival.
I didn't think
that I was giving up one life
to get another,
that even childhood
was full of sacrifice.
I'd just take the bright green thing,
pluck it off its only stalk,
and give it away as if
it were mine to give.
I knew someone out there
would be fooled,
that someone would accept
the precious gift.
So I just sent it along
with a plea of a prayer,
hoping it would spread its wings this time
and fly across that wet glass sky,
no concern for what inspired

its life, or mine,
only instinct guiding pain
towards the other side.

POEM FOR MY FATHER

I lie dreaming
when my father comes to me and says,
I hope you write a book someday.
He thinks I waste my time,
but outside, he spends hours over stones,
gauging the size and shape a rock will take
to fill a space,
to make a wall of dreams around our home.
In the house he built with his own hands
I wish for the lure that catches all fish
or girls with hair like long moss in the river.
His thoughts are just as far and old
as the lava chips like flint off his hammer,
and he sees the mold of dreams
taking shape in his hands.
His eyes see across orchids on the wall,
into black rock, down to the sea,
and he remembers the harbor full of fish,
orchids in the hair of women thirty years before
he thought of me, this home, these stone walls.
Some rocks fit perfectly, slipping into place
with light taps of his hammer.
He thinks of me inside
and takes a big slice of stone,
and pounds it into the ground
to make the corner of the wall.
I cannot wake until I bring
the fish and the girl home.

LAST
DAYS
HERE

WORKING CONSTRUCTION

In those days, I couldn't tell if I was strong.
But I survived our 60's style
rites of passage, every night till 2:00 a.m.
the sweet carcinogenic blend of Marlboros and pot,
the music and the bitter lick of alcohol
hardening our tongues for the coming years
of manhood, a still-soft first kiss
fading in a hotel lagoon.
And by dawn, a quick eggs and juice
and I'd shoot down to the E.E. Black job yard
to huddle in the back of a big green pickup
listening to Manuel steam our coffee
with stories of how many pregnant girls in P.I.
chased this manong clear out of his country,
and how many here are trying to send him back,
and him only laughing as we bounced our asses
down new stretches of freeway,
steel toes and dirt-stiff jeans and t-shirts
shivering in the first-light blues of Honolulu.
I was just a drop-out from college;
some of these guys were actually killers, con artists,
all kinds of thieves, ready to rip off
any small piece of reality.

For some, like Manuel, reality was talking girls
all day, even while waist-deep in a watercress patch
scooping out the foundations for the Waiau overpass,
a litany of tits, bilots, and erections
chanting us through whole mornings of mud.
As if for emphasis, he'd grab a big crayfish
off my shovel, rip off its mini-lobster tail,
and with a quick swish in a clean spot of water
down the delicacy with a whiskery grin,
tossing the waving claws and pointy nose
over his shoulders to the sky.

For Masa, who asked me to join his carpenters' union
to learn a skill, reality was slipping on his way
to the bathtubs he was installing,
and then falling three stories inside
the hollow new wing of Queen's Hospital.
He landed down where a sparse field
of steel re-bars was still standing 2 feet tall
out from the concrete foundation, waiting
for their next layer. He flew down
and got one through the wing,
missing his lung and heart, and months later
grinned and lifted his white t-shirt
to show me his scars.

There was the one I was afraid of,
I never knew his name, he was a Hawaiian
who had murdered his unfaithful wife.
Behind his black shades he must have
re-lived his pain, as he sat
alone in a heavy protective cage all day
shifting the gears of the tall crane
that swung the huge bucket, sloppy with concrete,
in a heavy arc up to the highest floors.

It was Big Charlie and me up there,
kids with a gigantic metal ice cream cone
filled with a quarter ton of grey mush,
him chuting it into the 8″ forms
while I stuffed it down before it stiffened,
backstepping in rhythmic strokes
7 stories in the air, with no railings,
no handholds, nothing but my shovel
keeping me balanced up there,
so lost in my confidence
and the steady flow of the pour, that in mid-stroke
I backed right off the end of the wall.

On one foot I tilted, shovel releasing,
the other foot lifting like a crane dying
in a tai chi pose, and Charlie reached around
and grabbed my arm and squeezed me back,
and for once I was glad to be skinny.
Take it easy, he said, 3 of the few words
he ever spoke to me.

Charlie took it easy.
Everyone knew how he primed himself each day.
Once I saw him take his rigs, jab himself,
and then jam 7 hours straight
on a jackhammer, alone, cracking
old walls to dust, covering himself
with powder till he glowed
like the angels that blasted him
through his brief eternity.
Lunchtimes, in the parking lot,
safe and resting in the octopus roots of a banyan tree
he was dealing the stuff, heroin;
and all I could think was, he saved me.

The last job site that year was in Hell
or maybe Purgatory, I don't know which
is a flat, salty, crushed-coral plain in Ewa
where no trees, no wind, no sound exist,
except for the rippling 90 degree heat
that can pulse the sweat from your face.

It was a graveyard for used forms
flaking the concrete from their last wall,
all sizes of iron scaffolding, their heavy
H-frames rubbing off some of your palms,
and 4 by 8 plywood warping their last layers
as they were washed and stacked
for their next incarnation.

We were like boys gathering our Tinkertoys,
counting up how many we had of each piece,
although, in reality, we didn't care
cause we never got to construct our own fantasies.
And it was so hot we worked for 30 minutes,
then took breaks in makeshift shade,
sucking water from a cooler.
One guy always went for long shits
in the SANITOI, a risky place
to open a zipper with dozens of scorpions
keeping time on the walls.
One day somebody peeked in,
found him giving himself a dirty handjob,
desperate for a little ecstasy in the dim,
stinking closet of his little heaven.

THE IMMIGRANT

they knew
she was naturally dark
under the working tan
they knew
thick eyebrows were grown
to shade the sun
or catch the sweat
as with gloves and hoe
clearing land
she worked
her body
they said was made
for a field

under the brim
of her hat
her eyes stared at the ground
like two lost stones
after rain

she stands
a curved stem in the wind
over those rows of thin leaves
she keeps the corners of the hoe
chipping the unwanted green from the field
and as she works toward the tool shack
leaning on the horizon
she sees in its corrugated roof and wooden walls
the ship of her dreams
holding sky

weed by weed she pulls her way
each stroke of the hoe
notching the earth ocean
waiting for when she can walk

the rest of her life
into the cool rectangular boat
and sail across those green latitudes
eating lunch at the window
as whole nations pass by

POEM FOR GEORGE HELM:
ALOHA WEEK 1980

I was in love with the word "aloha"
Even though I heard it over and over
I let the syllables ring in my ears
and I believed the king with outstretched hand
was welcoming everyone who wanted to live here
And I ignored the spear in his left hand
believing instead my fellow humans
and their love for these islands in the world
which allow us to rest from the currents
and moods of that vast ocean from which we all came
But George Helm's body is back in that ocean
I want to believe in the greatness of his spirit
that he still feels the meaning of that word
which is getting so hard to say

I thought there was hope for the word "aloha"
I believed when they said there are ways
in this modern technological world Oahu alone
could hold a million people
And we would become the Great Crossroads of the Pacific
if we used our native aloha spirit
our friendly wahines and our ancient hulas
They showed us our enormous potential
and we learned to love it
like a man who loves some thing in gold or silver
But these islands are made of lava and trees and sand
A man learns to swim with the ocean
and when he's tired he begins to search
for what he loves, for what will sustain him
George Helm is lost at sea
The bombing practice continues on Kahoolawe
I want to believe in what he was seeking
I want to believe that he is still swimming
toward that aina for which he feels
that word which is so hard to say

I want to believe in the word
But Brother George doesn't say it
He doesn't sing it in his smooth falsetto
in the melodies of aloha aina
There is no chance of seeing him walk up to the stage
pick up his guitar and smile the word at you across the room
The tourists, they twist their malihini tongues
The tour guides mouth it with smog-filled lungs
Politicians keep taking it out, dusting off the carcass
of a once-proud 3 syllable guaranteed vote-getter
You find its ghosts on dump trucks, magazines
airplanes, rent-a-cars
anywhere they want the dollar
They can sell you anything with aloha and a smile
even pineapples that they brought here from
(you guessed it) America!
They'll sell you too, servants of the USA
And if you don't believe they have the nerve
think of the ocean
They put up signs as close as they dare
And when his spirit comes back to land
the first thing he'll see is a big sign with that word
painted on, carved in, flashing with electricity
That word, so hard to say

I was going to believe that word
I was going to believe all those corporations
that seemed to spring up like mushrooms after a light
rain
I was going to believe when they divided up
the home-land of a living people
and called it real estate, or 50th state
or, Aloha State
I was going to believe we would still be able
to go up to the mountains, out to the country beaches
So many trying to swim in the waves

legs kicking, arms paddling like the arms
of George Helm stroking towards a familiar beach
which he respected and belonged to by birth
for which he felt something no word can express
except for that word which is hard to say
unless we all live it

I want to live the word "aloha"
But the body of George Helm is lost at sea
the practice continues on Kahoolawe
the buildings follow the roads
the roads carry thousands of cars filled with people
following their dreams of Hawaii or Paradise
to Waikiki where girls sell their hips
singers sell their voices
the island which has been sold is lit up all night
while the king with outstretched hand
has forgotten how to use his spear
George Helm is dead
and that word
it rings in my ears every day
I want us to live the word "aloha"
but it's so hard just to say

QUESTIONS FOR A MODERN DAY ICARUS

1

I got used to watching you try
to make the fast section of the wave
breaking over the coral beds we called Shallows,
even after that time I saw you lift
your shredded chin from the water,
a red beard dripping down your chest.
That was your style.
At least, that's the recollection I get
everytime that last dive you took
recurs in my dreams,
your clenched jaw grimacing
before the asphalt parking lot
forces your spirit
out of your face and flesh.

2

Was the rug too soft,
the window, the sky, too open,
only your shadow
pulling you back into the room
as you leaned
for a closer look?
How can I forget your footprints
in the carpet?
How can I feel your grip
at the sill
without wanting to follow
your flight toward heights greater
than a seventeen story high rise,
your soft gaze hardening only
when gravity forced your eyes
toward concrete?

3

The grit of your teeth
is all I recall.
There is no impact
to complete the act.
Only this: the funeral casket
open to our procession
where you lie straight-faced
beside your weeping mother
until I reach you,
then you open your eyes
and say to her, okay,
he came, we can go now,
and you climb out
and walk away, leaving
me with the empty box.
What's the message?
Did you know why I was late,
almost missing your last show?
Did you know how all these years
I've been contemplating
the freedom you were seeking?
And did you know
the only thing that keeps me here
is the belief that we can learn
and will probably come back
to this world, as usual,
until we know
we need no more.

PAPIO

This one's for you, Uncle Bill.
I didn't want to club the life
from its blue and silver skin,
so I killed it by holding it
upside-down by the tail
and singing into the sunset.
It squeaked air three times
in a small dying chicken's voice,
and became a stiff curve
like a wave that had frozen
before the break into foam.

In the tidal pool
we used to stand in
I held the fish and laughed
thinking how you called me
handsome at thirteen.
I slashed the scaled belly,
pulled gills and guts,
and a red flower bloomed
and disappeared with a wave
like the last breath
your body heaved
on a smuggled Lucky Strike and Primo
in a hospital bed.
You wanted your ashes out at sea
but Aunty kept half on the hill.
She can't be swimming the waves at her age
and she wants you still.

MANOA CEMETERY

for Moi Lum Chock, 1975

1

I am late as usual
but no one makes an issue of my coming.
Candles are lit and incense burns
around the stone.
The rituals have begun.
We offer five bowls of food;
bamboo shoots and mushrooms
we've cooked for you today.
And there are five cups of tea
and five of whiskey
to nourish and comfort you
on your journey.
It's been a long year since you left,
and for me, the sense of regret
deepens into mystery.
It is not strange that we miss
your gracious presence,
your good cooking, or good smile;
but as we all take our turns
to bow and pray before your grave,
I begin to wonder who you are.

2

I feel silly
to think I follow custom
pouring you a sip of whiskey
I never saw you drink.
But when I kneel before your stone,
clasp my hands, and bow three times,
I remember how you taught me prayer
before your parents' ashes
stored in earthen bowls

in a sacred room.
They've since been moved
and now they're buried
with a proper stone
just one row up from you.
You know others on this hill.
We give them incense too.

3

It was many years earlier
that an old Hawaiian king
offered a friendly Chinaman
all the land from Waikiki clear up Manoa
to this sacred hill
where we stand or kneel in worship
as our grandparents taught us to do.
The old man refused,
saying, just give me enough
to bury my people.
I wonder if the Chinaman knew
what he was saying?
Even you, two generations before me,
were not born in China
but I think near Hanalei.
So what is it gains a place
among these laborers, merchants, tailors?
The repetition of names
sprawls across the hillside
and I remember once
I thought I saw a baby
in my lover's eyes.
Now I keep an endless pain
regretting great-grandchildren
that were lost. Forgive me.

I cannot name the reasons.
And if you
who put your earthly life
in taro and sugarcane
deserve a burial and worship on this hill,
I should have my ashes scattered
from an airplane.

4

But today we wash your stone,
trim the grass around your plot,
and it is for you we sanctify
this world
with food, flowers, and firecrackers.
The sound and sulfur smoke
drive evil spirits away
as we burn gold paper
folded into money.
Now it's time to go,
but we'll return every year—
a gathering of tears,
and rituals of fire.

MEETING OLD FRIENDS DOWNTOWN
BY ACCIDENT

Poor things, Violet and Maka,
got nothing better to do on Wednesday
than smell Sotelo's chicken adobo
curling upstairs into their noses
and tickling their intestines.
Never mind Violet's leg and back
operations in the last six months,
Maka's one eye gone blind
since we saw each other
Old Vineyard Street.
Maka say to me, "Anytime you gotta
get your health back quick,
just eat plenty, get fat!"
Guarantee they believe,
they go down the New Dalisay Cafe
buy the best Filipino food,
tell us about the times hospital
when they say they both was skinny,
couldn't get out of bed,
but now they keep their
Hawaiian-style insurance
tucked tight in their skins,
that extra cushion they carry around
for the next hard time.

Our okoles slide sideways
out from the wooden booths,
cruise down Maunakea Street
re-living nights at the Shindig,
the Aloha Grill, Hawaiians
moonlighting their music in clubs
that come and go between porno stores,
fights exploding here and there
while we tell ourselves about safety
and beer bottles and the way things change
or move away, or new management,

re-development such a strange word
to the people who feel their age
disintegrating with the old buildings
being demolished around them.
Looking for a crack seed store
on the way to the open market,
Maka's one eye going wild checking
to see what's still in place,
she calls to us, "Why so fast?!"
She was right.
Only one more block and
hugs on the sidewalk good-bye.
Maybe seven more years before
we meet again.

TUTU ON DA CURB

Tutu standing on da corna,
she look so nice!
Her hair all pin up in one bun,
one huge red hibiscus hanging out
over her right ear,
her blue Hawaiian print muu muu
blowing in da wind
as one bus driver blows
one huge cloud of smoke
around her,
no wonder her hair so gray!
She squint and wiggle her nose
at da heat
and da thick stink fumes
da bus driver just futted all over her.
You can see her shrivel up
and shrink little bit more.
Bum bye, she going disappear
from da curb
foreva.

PUA'A: NUUANU

It was
in a voice
I couldn't understand
in a language
I didn't know.
I sat in my car listening
to the pua'a
the wild black pig
that had jogged
out of the shadows.
I slowed
to let him pass
on this quiet curve
in the mountains
where suddenly the sunlight
hitting asphalt
was louder than my idle engine.
When he turned and charged me
the violent thump on my bumper
was like a war cry.
It was his way
of screaming at my machine.
After having his say
and slightly dizzy now
after probably his first encounter
with civilization
he wobbled up the road
his furry black balls bouncing
between his legs
like bells.

HEIAU

Starting anywhere,
the form of the wall
is so clear
that stones slide
back into place
almost of their
own will.

Some fall back
around our bare feet.

But by the end of day
we find a place
for each.

This is our
worship.

When we leave,
we carry the shapes
of lava
like prayers
in our hands.

CHINESE FIREWORKS BANNED IN HAWAII

for Uncle Wongie, 1987

Almost midnight, and the aunties
are wiping the dinner dishes
back to their shelves,
cousins eat jook from the huge vat
in the kitchen, and small fingers
help to mix the clicking ocean
of mah jong tiles, so the uncles can play
through another round of seasons.
And you put down your whiskey
and go outside to find your long bamboo pole
so Uncle Al can help you tie on
a ten foot string of good luck,
red as the raw fish we want
on our plates every New Year's.
As you hang this fish over the railing
Uncle Al walks down the steps
and with his cigarette lighter
ignites it and jumps out of the way.
You lean back and jam the pole
into the bottom of your guts,
waving it across the sky,
whipping sparks of light from its tail,
your face in a laughing Buddha smile
as you trace your name in the stars
the way we teach our kids to do
with their sparklers.
This is the family picture
that never gets taken, everyone
drawn from dishes and food and games
and frozen at the sound
of 10,000 wishes filling our bodies
and sparkling our eyes.
You play the fish till its head explodes
into a silence that echoes,
scattering red scales to remind us of spirits
that live with us in Hawaii.

Then, as we clap and cheer,
the collected smoke of our consciousness
floats over Honolulu, as it has
each year for the last century.
But tonight, as we leave,
Ghislaine stuffs her styrofoam tea cup
full of red paper from the ground.
This is going to be history, she says.
Let's take some home.

WHAT? ANOTHER CHINESE HOLIDAY?!

Moon Festival again,
black sugar cakes ruined
with old egg yolks.

No fireworks to
blow me away.
No lion dancing.

Just some folks
hyping old ways
to make a buck.

Who cares what
harvest the moon
shines on?

Where's a tv?
I wanna watch
the World Series!

Full moon?!
I don't even know
when it is.

If it's round
and white
in the October sky

it's gotta be
a home run,
cracking the American

night.

STRAWBERRIES

Leave me alone.
I'm just an ordinary man
who loves strawberries.
I love to grab the green fuzziness
in my gathered fingertips
and dip the seedy point in sour cream
and brown sugar
and into my waiting lips.
Mmmm, that's a sweet kiss worth
repeating all night,
just an ordinary man
loving his strawberries.
And I don't want to have to think
who picked them with
what brown illegal alien fingers,
back bent under the California sun
that used to belong to his forefathers anyway.
I don't wanna know that the price of cream
is American decadence that the rest of the world
would never dream of spending,
or that sugar is giving me an insulin rush
or that the strawberries were sprayed with EDB
causing me cancer.
I don't wanna know these things
so don't bother me!
I'm just an ordinary man
who loves strawberries that come to me
past striking cashiers at Safeway,
that come to me in green plastic baskets
that will not decompose, but fill the air
with toxic fumes as they're incinerated
in the city dump polluting Hawaii's air and ocean,
plastic containers, a petroleum by-product
that the Arabs are processing
to enable the rich to buy the homes
of movie stars in Beverly Hills,

to buy whole hotels in Miami
or L.A. or New York,
while the rest of their people in poverty pray,
bowing their heads to the ancient ground
while all the oil flows out of the deserts
to America to grease the great machine
that grows the strawberries that I love,
sent by diesel trucks to the coast,
and by jet to Hawaii
where I can sit on my bed
and enjoy the pleasures of an ordinary man,
kissing that sweet kiss all night long,
without a care in the world.

LAST DAYS HERE

The wrinkle-faced man
chews his cigar, watching for direction
as he spits his left-over juices
downstream toward the harbor.
Almost forgetting the hot sun
and the fishing story
he told his wife and himself
this morning, he lets
the river pull his line,
the wind comes up to meet his eyes,
and his hands are content
with memories of fish in them.
He doesn't care
his fingernails stink
from baiting hooks with shrimp,
the time passes that way,
the tide reaches for his feet,
he doesn't care, he hangs them
from the wall for nothing.
Clouds stand up like huge trees,
he looks toward the sky
as if it was a clock,
and walks home thinking
his work is well-done.
The empty bucket stares a moment
toward his brain, so he closes
the closet door, hums
the ashes off his cigar,
and goes in to dinner.
He will never forget his days here.
In the dirt under the mango tree
prints of chicken feet
go every which way.

HOME
FREE

IV

HOME FREE

I am like my father
who never left Hawaii,
working the dry docks at Pearl,
sending the ships back
to find their purpose
near some foreign port
or out at sea.
He would rather go home after work
to the quiet place beside the stream.
He'd take his cane knife
to the mango tree,
then have me bundle the branches
while he raked or mowed
or weeded the lawn
to one pure green.
He used to say to me,
"What you gonna do next week
if the grass don't grow back?"
Back then, I couldn't see
the sense of his cycles,
what freedom we could find
in belonging to our subtle seasons
of mangoes, lichee, or monkey pod
beans and then leaves.
But now, I stand beside
what used to be our stream;
the smell of grease or garbage reeks.
The influx of certain birds
limits the number of mangoes I can eat.
Even the tv, where he used to say,
"Come quick Mommy, we can go to Paris,
for free!"
is no longer clear enough
without a cable hook-up,
so fenced in are we
with condominiums walking up from town,

into our valley.
Now that I've grown up, and gone away,
I want to develop my own sense of green.
I want to be able
to cup my hands in a clear stream.
All I want
is to be home free.

AND MORE

This one came from red dirt Kauai.
A whole camp of dusty kids
trying to bathe in a backyard tub.
She came from a bunch of wide
Nisei eyes floating in the front step portrait
of the wooden plantation shack
peeling its way behind them into the ground.
Throw her in a muddy irrigation ditch,
she'll kick and learn to swim like the rest.
She can weed the garden with Old Black Joe,
gather eggs to the tune of Dixie,
start the back porch hibachi fire singing
Swing Low, Sweet Chariot.
She can read by the light of a kerosene lamp
like Lincoln.
She can swear if you give her bullshit.
She can curl her hair and smile
in a high school portrait still hanging
in the hall at Waimea,
her eyes flashing back at the camera
dreams rooted sweeter than acres
of Hawaiian sugar cane.

She can leave home for Honolulu
to clean haole houses and graduate college
in the middle of a war;
teach kids to Speak American;
be a social worker to Filipinos giving her
ong choi grown in water that flows
under their houses, or to Samoans
weaving feathered fans for her
to bring home to her growing family,
her husband working Pearl Harbor to support
their version of the American Dream.
She can raise kids who are studious,
hippies, Born Again, or never home,

before settling down with doctors, lawyers,
computers, and families of their own.
And then there's still the one writing
all this down, trying to hold some kind
of mirror back to those eyes,
reflecting sweeter dreams than just
red dirt, even in Hawaii,
can grow.

HANAPEPE BON DANCE

for Ghislaine, 1986

After dinners of fresh uku and ono
at the Green Garden with this one
who wants to see where my mother is from,
we walk into the carnival lights
of the Zenshuji Bon Dance
honoring the return of departed souls.
The old singers climb the central tower,
lean on the rail of the platform,
and wail their wrinkled voices down to us
circling around, the dancing drummers
in turn, kicking, twisting, and
pausing on the backswing before
taking a deep stroke into the one big drum
that vibrates the dancer in us all:
farmers, businessmen, housewives, teachers,
tourists, a town breathing in unison
its common life.
As I squeeze my lover's hand I wonder,
Have I left this behind?

Tracing the same red dirt circles
every summer of their lives,
Nisei women in kimonos
bend and step, and release
their working hands like a flock
of cranes flying above their heads,
an inner circle of sansei and yonsei girls
following their movements,
the men with folded arms
watching the procession
of mothers and aunties, sisters and cousins.
Their food booths feed the crowd,
the baseball throw and ring toss
keep their teenagers near,
helium balloons of silver or gold,
some shaped like red-scaled fish,

escape the grip
of their children's hands
and capture everyone's attention
before disappearing into the night sky.
The drum beat becomes our inner rhythm
as the night progresses toward a belief
in a history which tonight is performed
like a live movie for my lover and me.
Can she see us young,
giggling shyly over Cokes
in a dark corner by the fish pond?
Or as dancer and singer
repeating the moves we practice
to perfection all our lives?
Or as the old couple in the temple
who spend the night tending the altar,
keeping the incense burning?

We leave past the pine tree
with its fuzzy punk bonsai haircut,
look back through the last open panel
of the wall of shoji doors.
In the temple light we see
the relaxed pose—one arm resting
on one raised knee—the Buddha,
at home, on Kauai.

GHISLAINE'S QUILT

The first sketches came when I was away.
I don't know if it started
more from her dream
or the real volcano she owns
a piece of, which recently
overflowed the roads
to the sea.
But the quilt I look down
every night in bed
is a patchwork mountain
of blacks and greys like different
days of cooling lava,
abstract shapes like burnt
leaves scattering, and gobs of red
paisley oozing fat tears
from the open mouth
which seems to be
waiting for stars to fall
from the squares of sky.
Sometimes I'm at the peak,
underneath the sky in my sleep.
Sometimes I'm receiving the red flow
into my mouth, which, she says,
always opens when I dream.

DEUX LANGUES

You say let's go "at my house"
as your translation of *à la maison*

You don't sweep
you "broom" the room

You want to buy a "nasal"
for the garden hose

I try to correct your English
but then you have "the taste for kissing"

and who can resist that kind of twisting
of our native tongues

URBAN GARDENING

1

While moving your rose bush
nearer the light
on our balcony,
thorns left pieces in my arm.

I left them there
like the pink petals
scattered on the rug,
as if I had arranged them.

2

One day, three
white cattleya orchids
with deep purple lips
and throats bloomed.
We moved them in,
first to the dining table
to enjoy with our meals.
Then we watched them uncurl
on top of the tv.
Later, we found their place
on our altar,
with our pictures of saints.
By then the petals were yellowing,
but, God knows,
they'd understand.

3

The *pikake* finally flowered
and hundreds of jasmine-scented stars

perfumed our bedroom.
In the dark,
while you brushed your teeth,
I piled the freshly-fallen
on your pillow.

MY FIRST WALK WITH ASHLEY

I can't understand any of your gurgling,
but when you raise your arm forward
and stare with raised eyebrows
beyond the opening and closing fingers
of your year-old hand,
I know I should follow that direction.
So with just one finger of mine in your grasp,
you lead me down the back stairs,
past the washing machine with its
audience of orchids and ferns,
and into the front yard.
You squat and smell some purple flowers,
giggling with complete pleasure.
Arm reaching again, we wobble out the driveway
toward the neighboring stream
where you know there are ducks,
one of the three or four words you know
besides mom and dad.
Your feet barely know which way is front,
so I've watched every step
just to make sure you don't fall.
Our path happens like a meditation.
Soon we are bending over the edge of the stone wall
trying to touch the water.
It's close enough.
We do it without having to get on our knees,
just by squatting again.
And the ducks are getting friendly.
You have already touched their wings as lightly
as if your fingers were feathers.
"Ducks," you say.
Now the white one that sits alone
is the one you want.
It runs away.
We pursue but can't get to it.
Once we got close.

It stopped and beat its wings as if
to lift off the ground
and you were in white feather awe,
your soft hands clasped together
as if in prayer,
your face in its light.
You're so young, but already
you know what you like.

MIYO'S JAPANESE RESTAURANT

It's part of the routine.
Maybe because the first time
they served me sashimi, the dish
was a crude, ceramic turtle
which read, "Save the Turtles"
when I reached the bottom.
And a heron waved its huge wings
as it landed, then hid,
among the long green fingers
of a coconut tree.
No matter why.

It happens every time.
It may be as I dip and lift
a pink piece of raw fish
with the tips of my wooden chopsticks,
rice bowl full and poised
in the left hand, ready
to catch a drip of green
wasabi-soaked shoyu;
or maybe it happens
as I begin to eat
the rice, which by now
has been dabbed enough
with tsukemono and fish,
and so is ready
to enter my lips.
Or it could happen
as I savor the last few
sips of miso, which I saved
on purpose, to wash down
this artfully prepared gift.

In any case, long before
the last drops of green tea
drain back into my cup,

I'll catch myself smiling
into the void which flashes
across my table, and while
nothing in particular
comes to mind—
even that pushes my smile
a few seconds more
into the Hawaiian night.

THE BODYSURFERS

We braid the red of sunsets
into each other's hair,
slip on our fins,
and enter between the waves
that soon surround us
like continuous thoughts
rippling that great mind.

From there, Oahu's blue green
mountains stand alert beyond
the hotel wall that divides us
from them, from our selves,
and if we paddle far enough
the buildings shrink to insignificance.

I love nothing better
than this glittering field
where I can watch you grip
the sides of your body board
like the shoulders of your lover,
as hugging it, you kick quickly
down the small slope, angle your face
away from the fine white spray
that stings your Canadian eyes shut
but still you go on, screaming for me
to echo, until we fade, and turn,
and before heading out again
laugh with our whole faces
releasing even the need
to be free.